THE NOTEBOOK OF DOOM

CHOMP OF THE MEAT-EATING VEGETABLES

by Troy Cummings

BRANCHES™
SCHOLASTIC INC.

TABLE OF CONTENTS

Chapter 1: RACK ATTACK! 1

Chapter 2: A SNACK FOR STELLA 9

Chapter 3: COOL SCHOOL 13

Chapter 4: CRY, CRY AGAIN 18

Chapter 5: JUST DESSERT 23

Chapter 6: A REAL PICKLE 29

Chapter 7: READY . . . AIM . . . SPLAT! 31

Chapter 8: LIGHTS OUT! 36

Chapter 9: THE NEW NURSE 42

Chapter 10: A CHILLING SECRET 49

Chapter 11: BIG, ORANGE, AND HUNGRY 55

Chapter 12: MR. MANNERS 62

Chapter 13: NEW SCHOOL 65

Chapter 14: PUMPKIN CELL 72

Chapter 15: TOSSED SALAD 80

Chapter 16: CHOP CHOP! 87

To Lisa, the awesomest sister in the whole county.

Thank you, Katie Carella and Liz Herzog, for helping me plot out the story, plow through the manuscript, and weed out the bad ideas to yield a peck of terrible, leafy monsters.

Library of Congress Cataloging-in-Publication Data

Cummings, Troy, author, illustrator.
Chomp of the meat-eating vegetables / by Troy Cummings.
pages cm. — (The Notebook of Doom ; 4)
Summary: Alexander is used to finding monsters everywhere in Stermont, but now the school is being turned into an icebox by giant meat-eating vegetables—and his friend Rip has gone missing.

(ebook) 1. Monsters—Juvenile fiction. 2. Elementary schools—Juvenile fiction. 3. Friendship—Juvenile fiction. 4. Horror tales. [1. Monsters—Fiction. 2. Schools—Fiction. 3. Friendship—Fiction. 4. Horror stories.] I. Title.
PZ7.C91494Ch 2014
813.6–dc23
2013027606

ISBN 978-93-5103-452-0

Book design by Liz Herzog

First Scholastic printing, January 2014

This reprint edition: April 2026

Printed in India

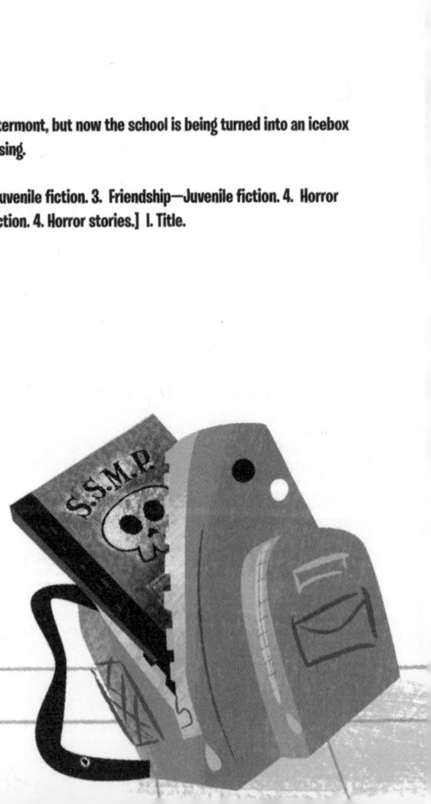

CHAPTER 1

RACK ATTACK!

"Are you ready for a surprise?" asked Alexander's dad, putting on an apron.

Alexander watched his dad chop a stalk of celery.

"That depends," said Alexander. "Does it involve vegetables?"

"Sort of . . ." said his dad. "You've been saying how strange the food is at school, so I decided we could start making your lunches at home."

Alexander thought about the weird meals they served at Stermont Elementary.

Alexander smiled. "Thanks, Dad."

"Now, why don't you clear off the breakfast table while I finish up here?" said his dad.

As Alexander was putting the milk away, he noticed a flyer stuck to the refrigerator door.

"Hey, neat,"
said Alexander.
"This Chili Supper sounds —"
He paused.
Something suddenly
felt . . . wrong.
He looked around
the kitchen.
The coatrack!
he thought.
*It definitely wasn't
here yesterday!*
It seemed to loom
over his father.

Some people may see a new coatrack and think nothing of it. But not Alexander Bopp. After moving to Stermont, he had learned two things:

1. His new town was full of monsters.

2. Everyday items — like coatracks! — could turn out to be monsters.

Alexander tiptoed up to the coatrack. . . . *Coats and hats? A perfect disguise!* thought Alexander. *But wait! Just to be sure, I'll look in the notebook!*

Alexander pulled an old notebook out of his backpack. He had found it on his first day in Stermont. It was filled with monster drawings. He flipped it open.

STICK FIGURE

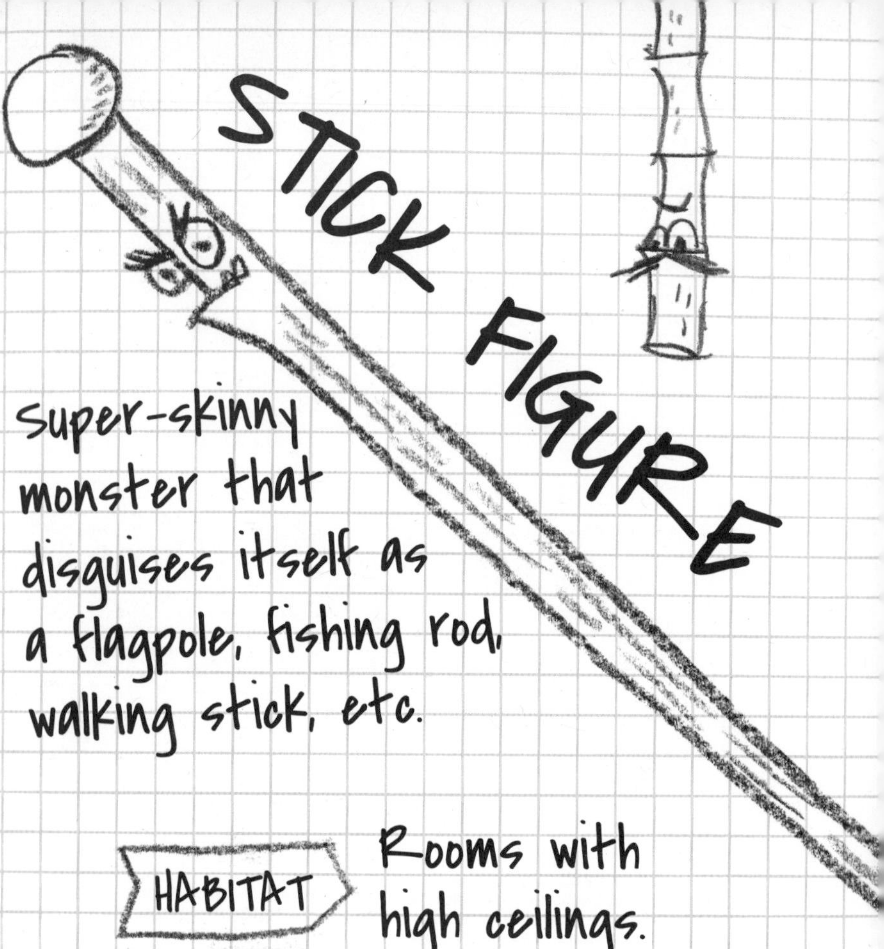

Super-skinny monster that disguises itself as a flagpole, fishing rod, walking stick, etc.

HABITAT Rooms with high ceilings.

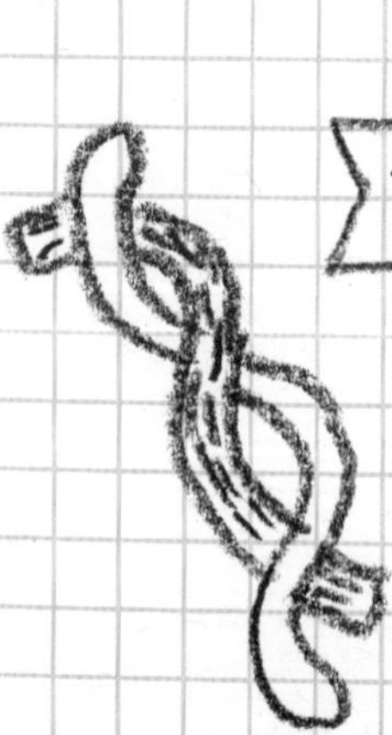

DIET Beef jerky and banana taffy, twisted into a long rope.

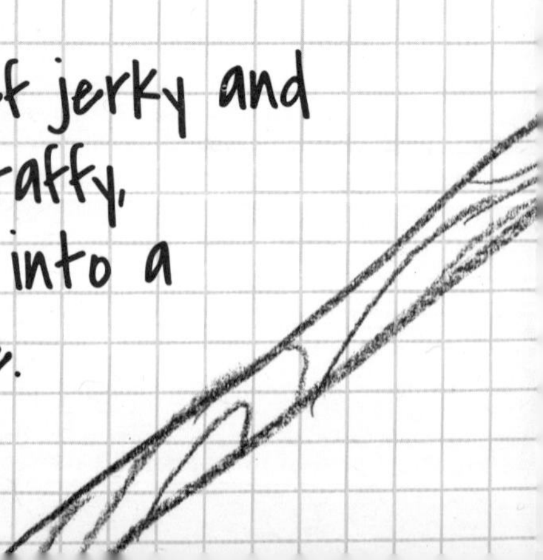

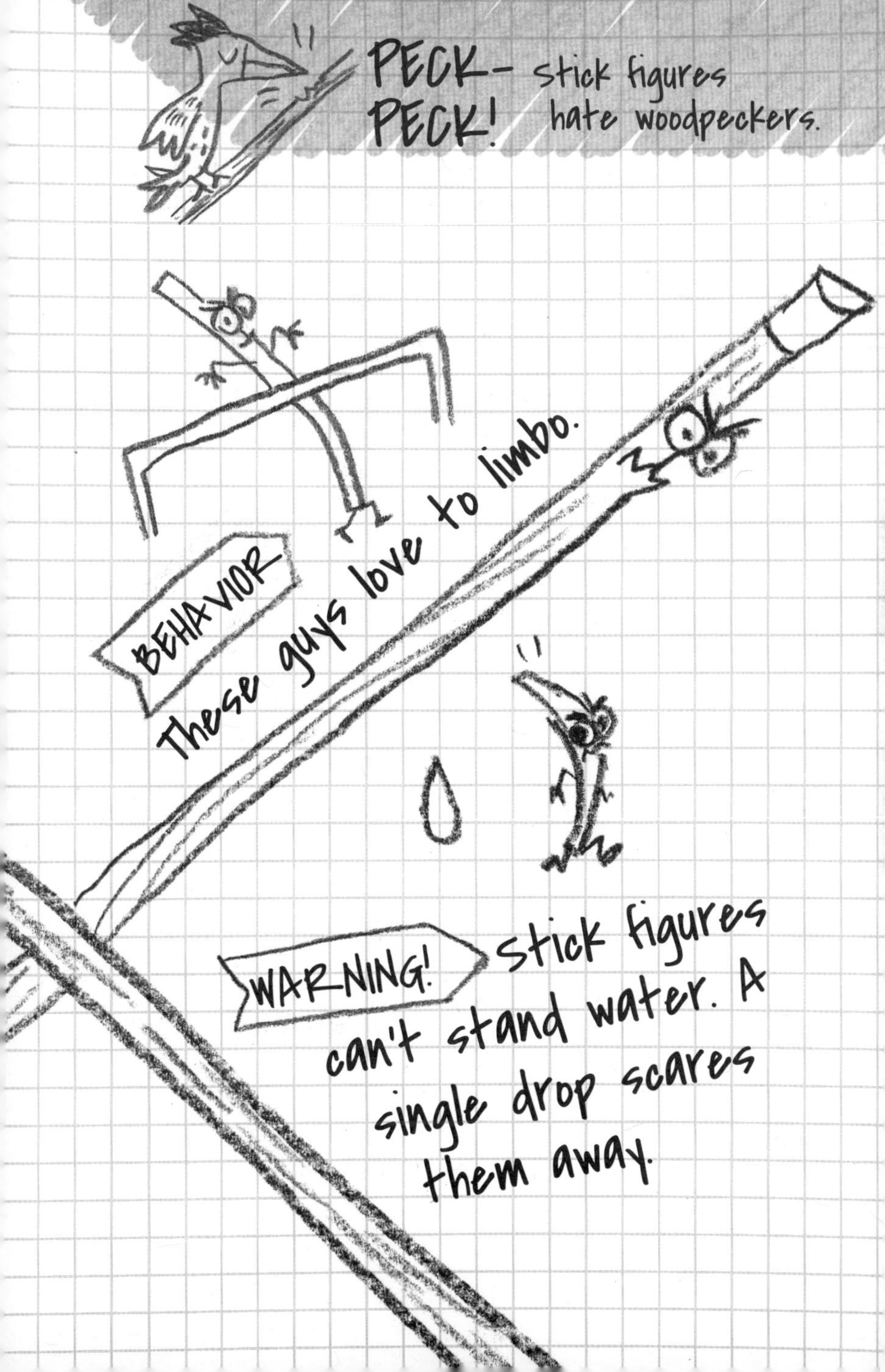
PECK-
PECK!
Stick figures hate woodpeckers.
BEHAVIOR
These guys love to limbo.
WARNING!
Stick figures can't stand water. A single drop scares them away.

"All right, kiddo! Time to —"

Alexander's dad turned to see his son leap from the counter, screaming a battle cry and snapping a wet dishtowel at the coatrack.

Alexander landed upside down in a pile of coats. The rack was still standing.

"Ah," said Alexander's dad. "You noticed our new coatrack." He helped Alexander to his feet. "I got it yesterday when I went shopping . . . for this!"

He handed Alexander a brand-new lunch box, fully-packed.

"Thanks, Dad!" said Alexander.

His dad winked. "You bet! Now, get to school!" he said. "I'll pick up these coats."

CHAPTER 2 A SNACK FOR STELLA

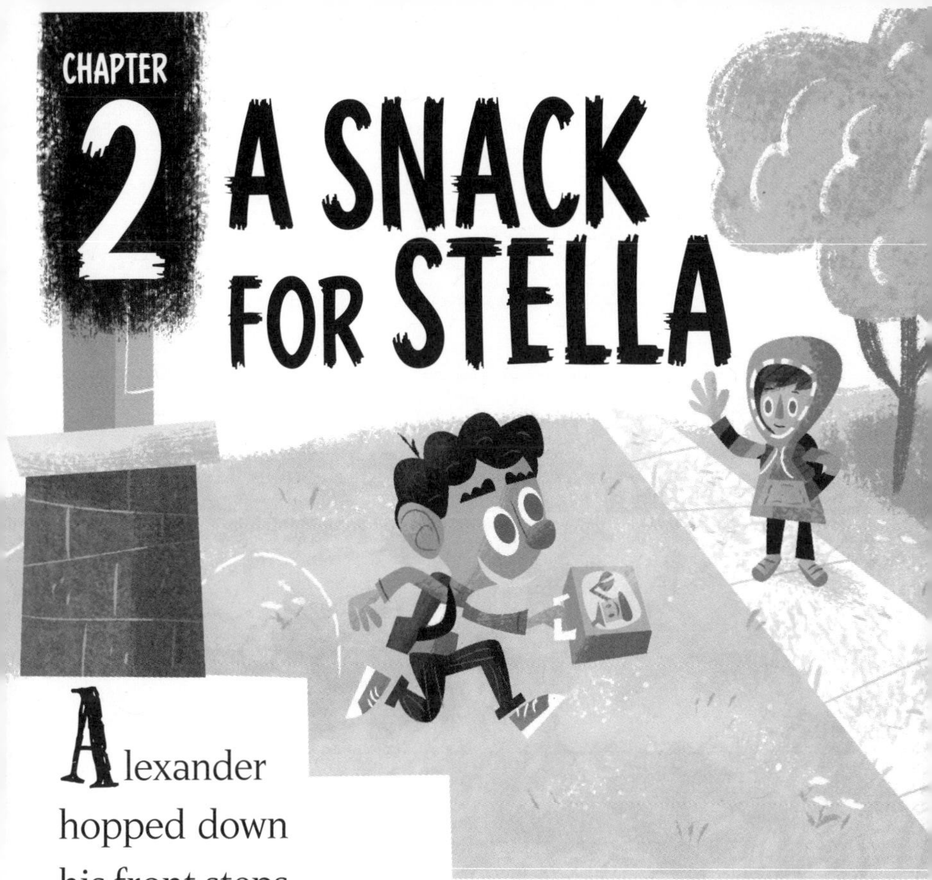

Alexander hopped down his front steps.

A girl in a hoodie waved to him from the sidewalk. "Hey there, Salamander!" she called. "Salamander" was Alexander's nickname. His teacher had called him that on his first day of school, and it stuck.

"Hi, Nikki!" said Alexander. He walked over to her, swinging his new lunch box.

Nikki leaned in. "Any S.S.M.P. news to report?" she whispered.

S.S.M.P. stood for "Super Secret Monster Patrol." The S.S.M.P. was a group of kids sworn to protect Stermont from monsters. Alexander and Nikki were two of the group's three members.

"Nope," Alexander said. "I thought there was a monster in my kitchen, but it was just a coatrack."

Nikki nodded. "Well, you never know when a big, ugly creature could show up."

"Hey, weenies!" barked a voice. "Wait up!"

A spiky-haired kid ran through somebody's flower bed to catch up with Alexander and Nikki.

It was Rip Bonkowski, the third member of the S.S.M.P.

“Guys,” said Rip. “Look what happened!”

He held up a broken skateboard. All four wheels had been mashed flat.

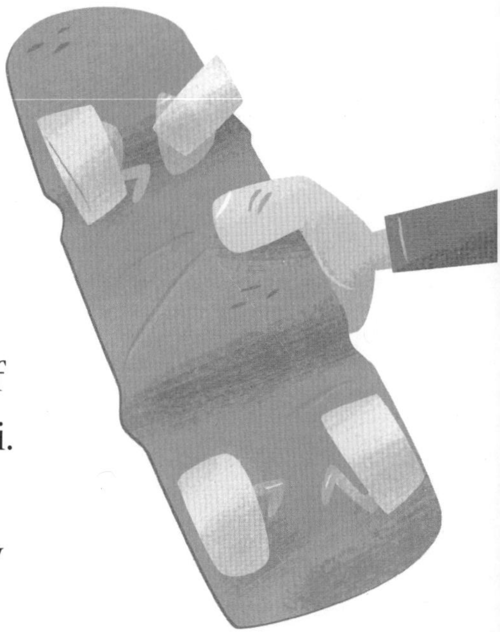

“Did you throw it off a building?” asked Nikki.

“*Huh?* No!” said Rip. “Something superheavy must’ve mashed it into the sidewalk. But I’d only stopped for a second to feed her!”

Alexander raised an eyebrow. “Feed who, Rip?”

Rip pulled a radish from his pocket. It was covered with nibble marks.

“Stermont Stella,” he mumbled.

"The gopher?" asked Alexander. "The one who dove into her hole to hide when those shadow smashers came to Stermont?"

"Yeah," said Rip. His cheeks turned redder than the radish. "Those shadow smashers really scared her! I've been stopping by Derwood Park every morning to bring her a snack. She needed a, um . . ."

"A friend?" said Nikki. She grinned. The sun sparkled on her braces. "Rip, did you actually do something nice for someone?"

"What?! No! Stella's just a gopher!" Rip threw his radish at Nikki. "And anyway, what about my smooshed skateboard! Who would do something so mean?"

"Maybe someone who doesn't like gophers," said Alexander, laughing. "Now, let's get to school."

CHAPTER 3

COOL SCHOOL

"Every time I come to this school," said Alexander, "I feel like I'm about to have my temperature taken."

"Yeah," said Rip. "It's creepy that our school used to be a hospital."

"Don't be such babies," said Nikki. "Anyway, the new school is almost ready. That's why Principal Vanderpants is having the big Chili Supper, so —"

BONK! Nikki crashed into the sliding doors. They hadn't slid open like usual.

"Look! The doors are frozen!" said Alexander.

Rip grunted as he yanked on the doors, forcing them apart. A big gust of freezing air blasted his face.

Alexander, Rip, and Nikki could each see their breath as they walked into the lobby. The walls were white with frost.

"Grab a coat!" shouted a tall man in a parka. He was handing out clothes from the Lost & Found.

"Mr. Hoarsely," said Alexander. "Why is it so cold in here?"

Mr. Hoarsely was the school secretary, gym coach, bus driver, and nurse. He was also a former member of the S.S.M.P, although he never wanted to talk about it.

"I'm not sure," said Mr. Hoarsely. He gave Alexander a sweater and ski goggles.

Alexander noticed icicles on the ceiling. *"Hmmm . . ."* he said. "This winter wonderland feels like the work of a monster!" He pulled out the notebook. "Maybe some ice mice, or a chill billy, or even a snombie!"

"Eep!" yelped Mr. Hoarsely, trembling. "Put that notebook away!"

Mr. Hoarsely handed Nikki a puffy jacket.

"I don't think this coldness is monster-related," said Nikki, pointing. "Look! The air conditioner must be broken."

An odd-looking man carrying a toolbox was heading toward the elevator. He wore a dark ski mask and overalls that read STERMONT A/C REPAIR.

"Brrrr!" said Rip. "Pass me a coat already!"

"Oh," said Mr. Hoarsely. "There's only one left." He tossed Rip a furry black-and-white snowsuit.

"I'm not wearing this!" Rip shouted.

"Ripley Bonkowski!" said an icy voice. The room grew even colder as an unsmiling woman drifted around the corner.

"Uh, hi, Principal Vanderpants," said Rip.

"The air conditioning may be stuck on full blast," she said, "but I will *not* have my students catch cold. You *will* dress warmly."

Rip looked at Alexander. Alexander shrugged. Nikki snorted.

"Okaaaay," Rip said, slouching. He pulled on the snowsuit and zipped it up.

"Perfect," said the principal. "You are now the fuzziest, wuzziest panda at Stermont Elementary. Off to class, you three!"

Rip started to growl, but it only made him look cuter.

CHAPTER

4 CRY, CRY AGAIN

Alexander wasn't sure he'd ever get used to having class in a morgue — an underground room where the hospital would stick dead people. But after several weeks of fighting monsters, a cold, windowless room was no big deal.

Alexander swung open the heavy door. "At least Mr. Plunkett likes to joke around," he said to Rip and Nikki. "Imagine how gloomy our classroom would —"

"WAAAAAAAH!" His teacher sat on his desk, crying into his hands.

"BOO-HOO-HOOO!" cried Mr. Plunkett. "Take a seat, Alexander."

Alexander adjusted his goggles. Every student in the classroom was sobbing — including Rip and Nikki.

"Are you guys okay?" asked Alexander. He sniffed the air. "And, hey, what's that smell?"

"Just sit down, weenie," Rip said between sobs. He stumbled to his seat.

Alexander followed Nikki to their table. She wept like a baby.

Why are they all crying? he thought. *There must be a monster behind this!*

He opened the notebook to a page speckled with old tear stains.

BLUBBER-DUCKIE

Rub-a-dub-RUN FOR YOUR LIFE!

SQUEAK! The blubber-duckie's song makes kids cry.

BEHAVIOR Blubber-duckies float alongside regular bath toys, waiting to be squeezed.

WARNING! Don't squeeze 'em unless you're ready to become duck chow. To survive: never take a bath.

Alexander closed the notebook.

"Well, blubber-duckies aren't making us cry," he said to Nikki. "They only hang out in hot baths. It's so cold in here that even my ski goggles are fogging up!"

Alexander gasped. *My goggles!* He pulled them off. Instantly, his eyes began to sting. Tears rolled down his cheeks. He snapped the goggles back into place.

HONK! Mr. Plunkett blew his nose. "Since you will be serving the grown-ups at the Chili Supper this Friday, we will spend the rest of the week studying table manners. You'll all learn how to be polite little waiters."

The class cried even louder.

That sharp smell, thought Alexander, rubbing his nose. *It's so familiar. . . .* "Nikki, I know that smell!" he whispered. "It's onions!"

CHAPTER

5 JUST DESSERT

"Yes! Lunchtime!" Alexander called back to Rip and Nikki. He dashed out of the elevator and into the freezing cafeteria.

Rip dabbed his eyes with his panda mitten. "What's the rush, Salamander? There'll just be something yucky on the menu."

"I came prepared!" said Alexander, jiggling his lunch box.

"Good thinking," added Nikki.

They stepped up to the menu.

"*Ooh.* Sorry, guys," said Alexander. "Hope you can choke down your re-re-re-refried beans while I'm eating a de-de-de-delicious, homemade lunch!"

The kitchen door swung open. A tall chef with short legs came out, carrying a wet sponge.

"Who's that?" asked Alexander. "He's not one of the regular cooks."

"How can you tell when he's all bundled up?" said Nikki.

Alexander shrugged.

The chef wiped the menu clean.

Then he wrote:

Alexander's jaw dropped.

Sure enough, there were several buckets of ice cream and dozens of toppings, beneath a sign that said **SERVE YOURSELF!**

"YES!" yelled Rip.

He gave Nikki a high ten.

"Find us a table, Salamander.
Nikki and I have some lunch to scoop."

Alexander shuffled over to a table and flipped open his lunch box.

Behind the note was a peanut butter, carrot, and celery sandwich. It looked like a bunny.

Alexander chomped a carrot. Then he shivered, but not because of the cold. The tall chef was glaring at him. Alexander swallowed.

The chef ducked behind a counter as a lunch lady stepped into view. She read the new menu, shrugged, and refilled the chocolate sprinkles.

BOOM! The table shook as Rip slammed down his mountain of ice cream.

Rip held his spoon high. "Never again," he said, "will lunch be *this* good." Then he dug in. Nikki sat down with a sundae of her own.

"Something's not right," said Alexander, "I mean, the super-cold school? That oniony smell? A new chef? And now ice cream for lunch?"

"You're just mad you brought your lunch on the one day they serve ice cream," said Nikki.

GROM! GROM! She scarfed down her sundae, splashing strawberry sauce everywhere.

"Nice table manners, you monster!" said Rip.

Rip wasn't joking. Nikki actually *was* a monster called a jampire.

Alexander and Rip had been surprised to learn that Nikki was a monster. But really, Nikki was more or less a regular girl.

She gave Alexander a big, drippy grin.

"How are your veggies?" she asked.

"Fine," said Alexander. He snapped his celery in half. **CRUNCH.**

CHAPTER 6

A REAL PICKLE

The next day, Stermont Elementary was even colder.

"Good morning, Salamander," said Nikki. She and Rip were bundled up near the classroom door.

"Hey," said Alexander. The onion smell had faded, but he snapped his goggles into place. Just in case.

"Ugh," said Rip, rubbing his tummy. "I overdid it yesterday with the ice cream. Next time I'll stop at eleven scoops."

"Hopefully today's lunch will be back to normal," said Alexander.

Mr. Plunkett bounced into the room. "Take your seats," he said. "Today's lesson: forks! If you're going to be good waiters tomorrow, you need to know your silverware!"

"Sheesh," Alexander whispered to Nikki. "I'm not looking forward to serving the grown-ups at the Chili Supper."

Mr. Plunkett tacked a chart to the wall. "Now, which fork is best for spearing a pickle?" he asked.

Alexander stared up at the chart. *I feel like a pickle, sitting in this crispy, cold, metal room,* he thought. *That's it! The whole school has been turned into one big . . . refrigerator!*

CHAPTER 7 READY... AIM... SPLAT!

Alexander spent the rest of the morning trying to convince Rip and Nikki that monsters were turning their school into a refrigerator.

"And look!" Alexander said as they stepped into the cafeteria. "The monsters even changed the menu again!"

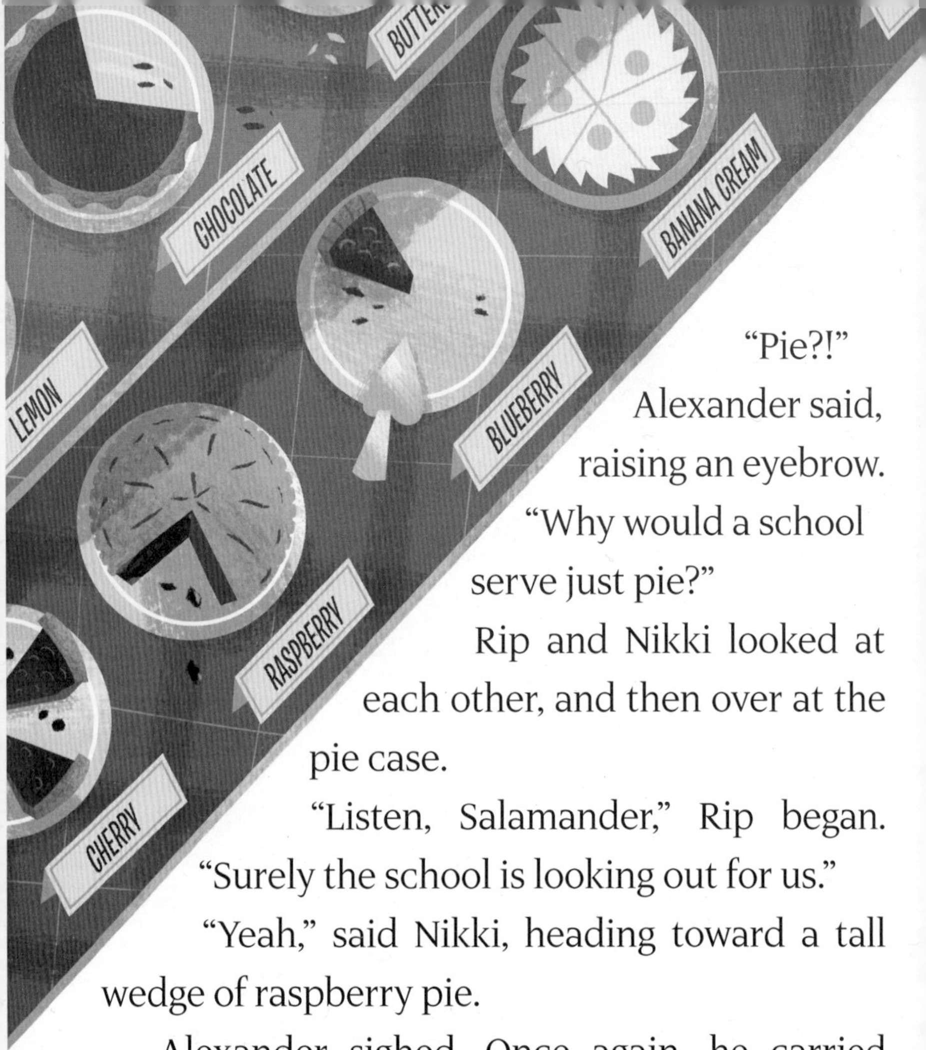

"Pie?!" Alexander said, raising an eyebrow. "Why would a school serve just pie?"

Rip and Nikki looked at each other, and then over at the pie case.

"Listen, Salamander," Rip began. "Surely the school is looking out for us."

"Yeah," said Nikki, heading toward a tall wedge of raspberry pie.

Alexander sighed. Once again, he carried his lunch box to an empty table to wait for his friends. He looked around. Everyone was chowing down on pie.

He flipped open his lunch box.

Beneath his dad's note was a veggie pita. Alexander took a bite as Rip and Nikki plopped down their trays.

"Watch me use my table manners," said Rip. He nibbled a bite of his blueberry pie.

"Manners? Ha!" said Nikki. She attacked her pie. Her plate looked like a crime scene.

"Here, Salamander," said Rip. "Try a bite!" He scooted his pie toward Alexander.

Alexander slammed his fist down.

"NO!" he barked. "There's something wrong here! School lunches should be *healthy*! Pie and ice cream for lunch is just . . . weird!"

He stood up and began shouting to the entire cafeteria, "I don't know why, but we shouldn't trust this pie! Am I right?"

Pie-stained faces stared back at Alexander. Rip began waving his arms.

"Sorry, Rip. You can't stop me!" Alexander said. He held Rip's pie above his head. "Even if no one believes me, I can't let you eat this pie! It's going in the garbage!"

He spun around and threw the pie.

Right into Ms. Vanderpants's face.

Silence fell over the lunchroom as clumps of blueberry rolled down the principal's coat.

Everyone could hear what Ms. Vanderpants said next, even though she spoke in a whisper.

"Alexander Bopp . . . see me after school."

Ms. Vanderpants stormed out, her face purple with anger — or maybe smooshed blueberry.

CHAPTER

8 LIGHTS OUT!

Rip shook Alexander's hand all the way to gym class.

"Salamander, you're my hero," he said. "A pie?! Right in Vanderpants's face?!"

"It was an accident!" said Alexander, pulling his hand free. "And I'm in huge trouble!"

"What will she do to you?" asked Nikki.

Alexander shook his head. "Whatever it is, it won't be good."

The friends filed into their school gym, which had been the old hospital's laundry room.

“I can’t wait for our new school to be finished,” said Rip. “Just imagine having gym in an actual gym. Instead of in *this* dump.”

Mr. Hoarsely stood near a clothes dryer, trying to untangle the cord on his whistle.

"Um, well, students," Mr. Hoarsely said. "Since the school's so cold, we won't change into our gym clothes today."

"Can we play dodgeball?" asked Rip.

"No way!" said Mr. Hoarsely. "It's dangerous to throw balls at other students! Let's play something safe, like tag."

Nikki snapped an icicle off a leaky pipe. "I think he means freeze tag," she mumbled.

Mr. Hoarsely checked his clipboard. "So I guess, when I blow my whistle, just . . . play tag."

The students began chasing one another. However, no one was "it." So they more or less ran in circles until — **CLUNK!** The lights went off. The room went dark. Students crashed into one another.

"Nikki!" said Alexander. "What's happening?"

"You can see in the dark, right, Nikki?" added Rip.

"Yes!" she shouted. "Come toward my voice!"

Something flew past Alexander's head.

"What was that?" he cried.

"It looked like . . . some sort of volleyball," said Nikki. "Watch out! Here come more!"

Alexander heard more balls whiz by.

"Dodgeball in the dark!?" Rip yelled. "This is awesome!" He ran off.

SPLAT! One of the balls hit a nearby kid. "Gross!" she said. "This ball's smooshy!"

"Salamander, jump left!" said Nikki. "Now, right!"

Alexander followed her directions.

"Now, catch!" called Nikki.

"Huh?" Alexander opened his arms and — **FLOMP!** — caught one of the balls. It was heavier than a volleyball. And slimy. And . . . moving! Alexander dropped it and felt it roll across his shoe.

"They're alive!" he shouted.

"Just get down!" said Nikki. "I'll go find the light switch."

Alexander dropped to the floor. He heard dozens of balls whooshing overhead.

BONK! BLAP! SPLAT!

Then, silence.

CLICK! The lights went on. There was no sign of the whizzing balls.

"Eep!" Mr. Hoarsely peeked out of the dryer.

All of the students had dropped to the floor, except one.

Rip wobbled in the middle of the room, covered in greenish goo.

Then he fell down.

CHAPTER 9 THE NEW NURSE

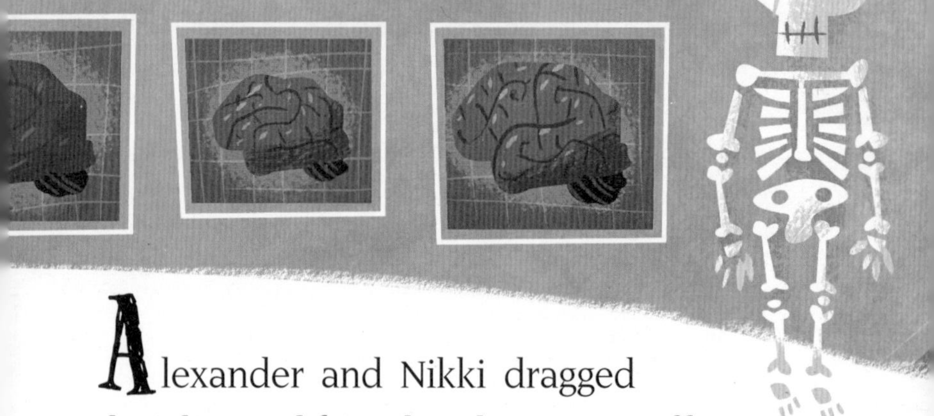

Alexander and Nikki dragged their bruised friend to the nurse's office.

The room was big. A fake skeleton hung near the door. At least Alexander hoped it was fake.

"There's one good thing about having school in an old hospital: We have an amazing nurse's office," said Nikki.

Alexander saw pictures of brains on the wall. "Looks like this used to be the brain surgery room," he said.

DING! Nikki rang the bell.

"Ughh," said Rip, lifting his head. "Why didn't Hoarsely just come with us? He's the nurse, right?"

"Hey, good point," said Alexander.

"He can't be everywhere at once," said Nikki. She looked at Rip's bruises. "So what were those balls that attacked us?"

Alexander dug out the notebook. "There's only one ball-shaped monster in here. . . ."

BLINKER

Your typical, everyday giant floating eyeball.

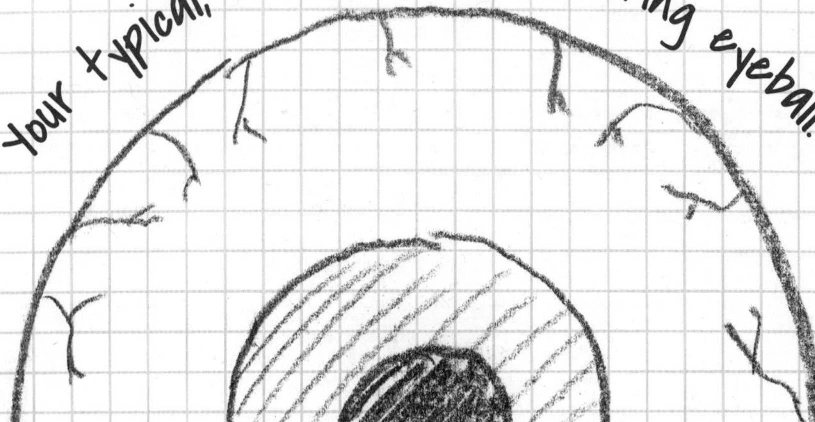

HABITAT Jewelry stores, car washes clean bathrooms. Any place with lots o shiny, sparkly surfaces.

LOOK! Blinkers always win staring contests.

DIET They feed on light and color.

BEHAVIOR Blinkers love bad TV. Especially game shows.

WARNING! Never look them in the eye! A blinker's gaze hypnotizes you. This makes it so you cannot peel your eyes away from boring movies you've already seen 40 times.

Alexander read the entry aloud. Then he turned to Nikki. "Could the balls that hit Rip have been blinkers?"

"No," said Nikki. "The balls were green and —"

"Oh, goodness!" said a sweet-sounding voice. "Is someone ill?" A large woman stepped into the room. A hairnet covered her bushy hairdo, and a surgical mask covered her face. Her nametag said NURSE BROCK.

"Our friend Rip is," said Alexander. "He got pounded by, um, dodgeballs."

"Oh, dear," said Nurse Brock. She leaned down and looked at Rip. "Tell me where it hurts. Are you tender here?" She poked him once in the ribs.

"*Ow!* YES!" said Rip.

NURSE BROCK

"Hmmm," said Nurse Brock. She looked down to Alexander and Nikki. "You children run along. I'll take care of this little pork chop."

When Nurse Brock's back was turned, Nikki whispered to Alexander and Rip, "Let's meet at S.S.M.P. headquarters after school. I saw something else in the gym that we should talk about."

"Okay," Alexander said. "But I may be a little late. I've already got an, um, appointment with the principal."

"Have fun," Rip said between moans. "See you at S.S.M.P. headquarters."

CHAPTER

10 A CHILLING SECRET

Alexander squirmed in his seat the rest of the afternoon. Then he rode the elevator to the coldest floor of the old hospital: the sub-basement.

He came to a door that said HEATING AND COOLING ROOM, with a sign tacked underneath: PRINCIPAL'S OFFICE.

He took a deep breath and knocked on the door. It swung open.

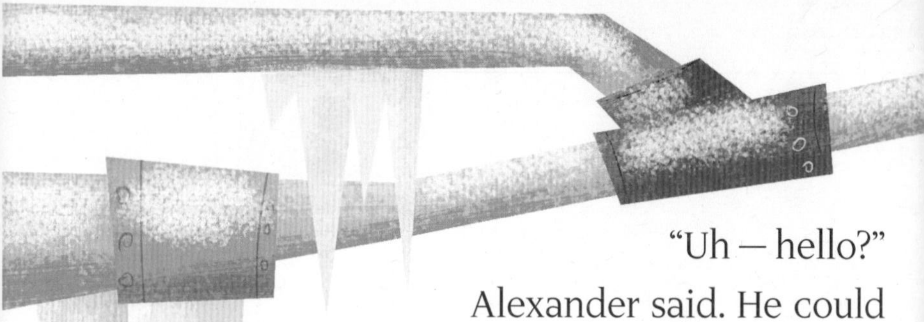

"Uh — hello?"
Alexander said. He could see his breath. "Ms. Vanderpants?"
She wasn't there. But there was a note.

Mr. Bopp,
Please wait. I will return.
-Principal Vanderpants

Alexander looked around. Low-hanging pipes crisscrossed overhead, branching out from a huge machine in the corner. The machine was shaking, humming, and covered in frost.

The air conditioner, thought Alexander. Then he blinked. Something purple and shiny — like a sheet of wrapping paper — was rattling around inside the machine.

TEMPERATURE
PEAS
MS. VANDERPANTS
PRINCIPAL

Alexander squatted down and pulled open a grate. The purple shiny thing blew out and drifted down into his hands.

Hmmm, thought Alexander. *This looks like* — he gave it a sniff — *a giant onion peel!* His eyes watered. *This is what was making everyone cry! I was right!*

Something else caught his eye: a small dial on the machine.

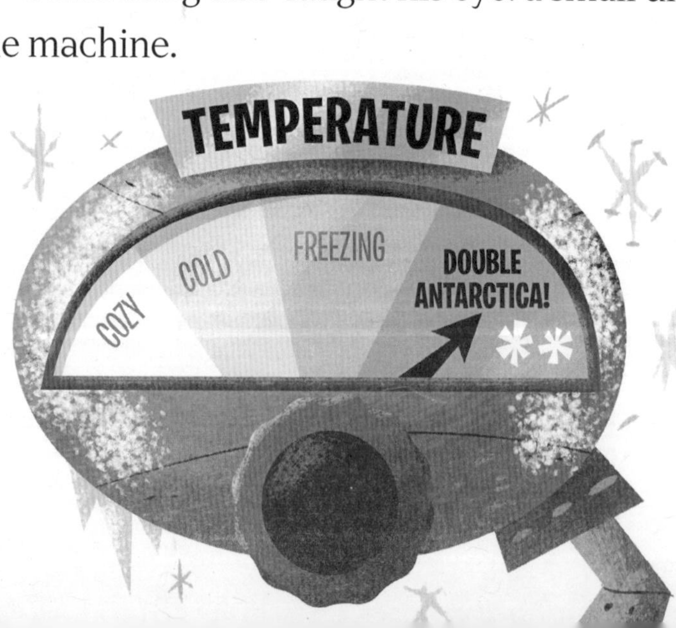

The air conditioner wasn't broken after all! thought Alexander. *Someone had set the dial to DOUBLE ANTARCTICA!* He turned the dial to COZY. The enormous machine shuddered, and went silent.

"Hello, Alexander."

Alexander jumped and hit his head on a pipe.

"Um, hello, Ms. Vanderpants," he said, jamming the onion peel into his pocket.

She stared at Alexander. Her clothes were stained with blueberry splotches.

Alexander cleared his throat. "I'm, uh, sorry about hitting you with that pie."

"Actually," said Ms. Vanderpants, "I should apologize to *you* for getting in your way."

Alexander wondered if he had bonked his head too hard.

"That's why I called you here," she continued. "I'm pleased to know you chose a healthy lunch over pie. And so I've made you Head Student Chef at the Chili Supper tomorrow."

Alexander's eyes widened. "But I can't cook!"

"Mr. Hoarsely will help," said Ms. Vanderpants. She began flipping through papers. "You may leave."

Alexander headed out the door, hoping Ms. Vanderpants couldn't hear the crinkly onion peel in his pocket.

CHAPTER

11 BIG, ORANGE, AND HUNGRY

Alexander ran through the woods behind his house. He couldn't wait to tell his friends about what Ms. Vanderpants had said and about the onion peel. The S.S.M.P. headquarters — an old caboose — was hidden in the woods. Nikki was already there, drawing in the dirt with a stick.

“Where’s Rip?” asked Alexander.

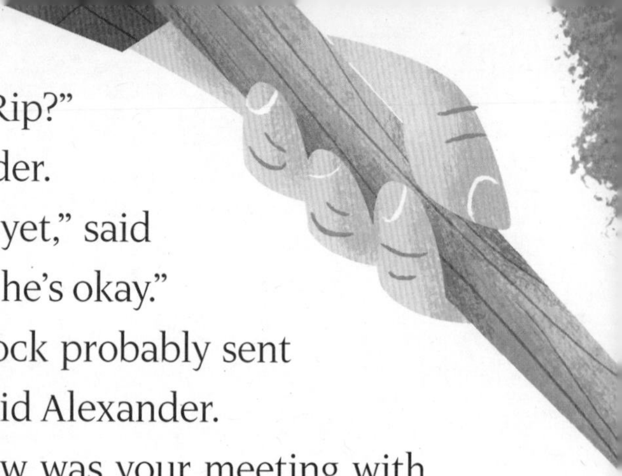

“Not here yet,” said Nikki. “I hope he’s okay.”

“Nurse Brock probably sent him home,” said Alexander.

“So . . . how was your meeting with Principal Vanderpants?” asked Nikki.

“You’ll never believe this,” said Alexander. “I’m not in trouble. In fact, she made me Head Student Chef for tomorrow’s Chili Supper.”

“Whoa!” Nikki said. “Speaking of ‘chef’ . . . That’s what I needed to tell you. . . . I saw who turned out the lights in gym class. It was our new chef — the one who changed the menu!”

Alexander frowned. “*Hmm,* I found something weird, too.” He showed Nikki the big onion peel. “This was in the air conditioner! And the dial was set to *DOUBLE ANTARCTICA*!”

Nikki drew a line in the dirt. “Okay, let’s make a list of what we know.”

Alexander looked at Nikki's list. She had drawn three circles in a row.

He gasped when he saw the circles. "Nikki! That's it! Pass me your stick!"

Alexander drew two arcs around the circles.

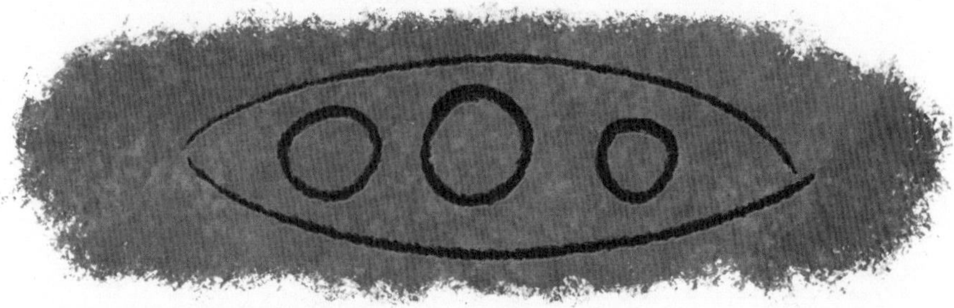

"Those balls were *peas*! Giant peas!" yelled Alexander. "And . . . the onion with a skin this size must be HUGE!"

Nikki narrowed her eyes. "You think we're up against *vegetable* monsters?"

"Yes!" said Alexander. "Veggie monsters must have lowered the temperature to turn Stermont Elementary into one big vegetable drawer! Like in a refrigerator!" He smacked his forehead. "Oh! Remember that round-looking repair guy? He must be an *onion*! That was *his* peel in the air conditioner!"

Nikki nodded. "That explains everything — except for the crazy lunches. Why is ice cream suddenly on the menu?"

"To fatten you up!" growled a voice.

Alexander and Nikki jumped back.

The new chef stepped into the light. He yanked off his hat. Green leaves sprung up.

"You're a carrot?!" asked Alexander.

"Yes!" said the carrot. "And I'm hungry! We plan to eat everyone at tomorrow's feast. But your tender friend said you'd try to stop us . . . so I felt like having a little pre-dinner snack!"

The monster tromped forward, flashing its pointy teeth.

Alexander threw his stick at the carrot.

The carrot laughed. "You can't hurt me with a stick! We don't feel pain — we're vegetables!"

Suddenly, the carrot froze in place. It began to tremble.

SHISSH-SHISSH.

A white rabbit peeped out from some nearby weeds. The rabbit sniffed the air, then hopped toward the carrot.

The carrot sprinted away.

Alexander and Nikki ran straight to Alexander's house.

"Phew!" said Alexander, between breaths. "We're lucky that rabbit showed up!"

"Yeah," said Nikki. "But it sounds like the veggies have Rip. What's our plan?"

"I'll study the notebook for vegetable monsters," said Alexander. He peered outside. "We'll make a battle plan tomorrow morning. Rip is counting on us."

"Hey, kiddos!" said Alexander's dad, popping into the kitchen. "Tomorrow's the big night! Ready to feed a bunch of hungry mouths?"

Alexander gulped.

CHAPTER

12 MR. MANNERS

Mr. Plunkett waited for his students to stop groaning. Then he plowed ahead with a third day of teaching table manners.

"Take out your napkins and start folding!" he said. "The Chili Supper is *tonight*!"

Alexander and Nikki sat in the back of the room, staring at Rip's empty seat.

"Do you think the veggies ate him?" whispered Nikki.

"No!" said Alexander. "Not yet — the carrot said they'd feast on us *tonight*! Let's go see Nurse Brock. She was the last —"

"Ahem!" Mr. Plunkett was standing right in front of Alexander. "What could possibly be more important than napkin-folding?" he asked.

"Er," Alexander said, "Well, Nurse Brock —"

"Who?" said Mr. Plunkett.

"Nurse Brock. Yesterday —"

"There's no Nurse Brock here," said Mr. Plunkett. "Hoarsely is the school nurse and —"

LISTEN UP!

Ms. Vanderpants's voice crackled over the loudspeaker. "Head Student Chef Bopp, report to the lobby. It's time to prepare the Chili Supper."

"Uh, that's me," said Alexander.

Mr. Plunkett's frown turned upside down. "Head Chef?!" he asked. "Use your table manners! Make us proud!"

Alexander swung his backpack onto his shoulders. "Hey, Nikki," he whispered. "Keep an eye out for Rip."

She nodded, frowning. "You know, I sort of, kind of miss that guy."

CHAPTER

13 NEW SCHOOL

On their way to the new school, Alexander and Principal Vanderpants passed a road sign that had been mashed against the sidewalk.

"Unbelievable," said Ms. Vanderpants. "Who would do such a thing?"

Veggie monsters! thought Alexander. The flattened sign reminded him of Rip's flattened skateboard. *Must've been a big monster!*

They soon arrived at the construction site. Alexander thought the new school — or what was completed of it — looked like a cross between a castle and a spaceship.

"What is that big glass room on top of the building?" Alexander asked.

"That's our greenhouse," said Ms. Vanderpants. "It's the only part that's finished. We'll grow food for school lunches in the garden up there, and we've got a plant lab for . . . important tests."

"Wow," said Alexander.

KITCHEN
COMING SOON
YOUR NEW SCHOOL!

Mr. Hoarsely stuck his long neck out of a nearby tent. "Okay, Alexander," he said. "Let's get started."

The two of them began setting up a kitchen in the tent.

"Mr. Hoarsely," said Alexander. "We don't have much time! Rip's been taken by these giant veg —"

"Whoa!" said Mr. Hoarsely as he handed Alexander a stack of napkins. "You're right! We *don't* have much time! These napkins won't fold themselves!"

Mr. Hoarsely seemed to be the only grown-up in Stermont who could see monsters. But he refused to talk about them.

"Now, then," said Mr. Hoarsely. "We have a chopping table and a big pot for the chili. We need —" He dropped his ladle.

"What?" asked Alexander.

"The *food*!" said Mr. Hoarsely. He threw open a cabinet, revealing hundreds of cupcakes. "I don't understand. The dinner food is missing — all we have is dessert!"

Alexander peeked out of the tent. "The parents are starting to arrive," he said. "And Principal Vanderpants is walking toward the stage!"

"Noooo!" Mr. Hoarsely cried.

Alexander dashed outside. His classmates were rushing around, setting tables.

Suddenly, the parents started clapping. Ms. Vanderpants had taken the stage.

"Welcome, parents," she said. "The money you have paid for this Chili Supper will let us move out of the old hospital building and into our new school!"

"The new Stermont Elementary will be 100% green," said Ms. Vanderpants. "We'll grow our food in the greenhouse, and use the wind from this windmill for our electricity!"

The tall curtain behind her fell, revealing a huge spinning windmill. Alexander saw his dad snap a photo. Then he saw something else.

Alexander tapped Nikki's arm. Then he pointed at the windmill.

"Yeah," said Nikki. "Those blades are huge!"

"No, Nikki," he said. "Look who's *behind* the windmill!"

It was Nurse Brock, rolling an enormous pumpkin.

CHAPTER

14 PUMPKIN CELL

"Nurse Brock is a vegetable monster?!" said Alexander.

"And I bet she's our Rip-napper!" said Nikki. "Let's follow her!"

They both ducked into the kitchen tent. Mr. Hoarsely was going crazy.

"Chef Bopp!" he cried. "We're *dooooomed*! We can't have a Chili Supper without chili!"

"I'm sorry, Mr. Hoarsely," said Alexander. "But we've got bigger fish to fry. I mean, vegetables to chop."

Alexander grabbed a carrot peeler and handed Nikki a potato masher. They snuck out the back.

“Where’d Nurse Brock go?” asked Alexander.

Nikki squatted down near some odd marks in the dirt. “Look! Pumpkin tracks!”

The tracks led to a metal staircase, which led up to the greenhouse.

“Come on!” said Alexander. “We’ve got to find Rip!”

They tiptoed up the stairs. It was warm inside — and misty, like a jungle. They hid behind a bush and looked around.

Nikki nudged Alexander. “I see the pumpkin!”

They crept through the plants to the middle of the greenhouse. The pumpkin had been carved like a jack-o'-lantern. But instead of a face, it had a window with bars on its front. A spikey-haired, square-headed kid sat inside.

"Rip!" shouted Alexander, running over. "Hang in there! We're going to bust you out!"

Rip shook his head. "Ugh! Really guys? Don't you know a trap when you see one?"

Nikki had been yanking on the bars, but stopped.

"What?" asked Alexander. "What do you — **OOF!**" A slimy green cannonball slammed into his back. Actually, it wasn't a cannonball.

It was a pea.

Then Nurse Brock stepped into the light, holding a large pea pod. She tore off her hairnet. She was a walking, talking stalk of broccoli. She snapped her fingers. And a dozen more vegetables sprung out of the garden.

"Since the beginning of time," said the broccoli, "we've been chopped, diced, pickled, or, worst of all, fed to your hamsters!"

The other vegetables growled.

"But tonight, we eat! We'll chomp adults, for forcing kids to eat us in the name of health! We'll munch kids, for using us as noses on their snowmen! And now, we'll eat you three for getting in our way!"

A giant potato fixed its twenty eyes on Alexander. "BUT FIRST, I'M GONNA MASH YOU SO YOU'RE SOFT AND TENDER!"

"Hey wait!" said Alexander. "It was *you* who mashed that crossing sign!"

"And my skateboard!" yelled Rip. He called over to Alexander and Nikki, "I should have listened to you before, Salamander. These are some tough veggies — NOTHING scares 'em."

"That's right," grumbled the carrot.

Alexander looked at the carrot, and then at Nikki.

"Are you thinking what I'm thinking?" he asked.

"For sure!" yelled Nikki.

Alexander dropped his peeler through the bars and whispered to Rip, "Peel your way out! Nikki and I will keep 'em busy! Head to the park — where your little friend is holed up — and bring her here! Hurry!" Rip started peeling as fast as he could.

Alexander and Nikki ran off, followed by an angry mob of mixed vegetables.

CHAPTER

15 TOSSED SALAD

As Alexander and Nikki sprinted through the greenhouse, Rip bolted from the construction site.

"Let's hide in there!" Alexander shouted to Nikki.

They squeezed into a patch of enormous sunflowers, each trying to catch their breath.

"BOO!" The broccoli peeked in.

Alexander and Nikki tumbled out, scratching up their arms.

"How are these monsters not getting tired?" Alexander said between breaths. "Rip had better hurry back!"

The greenhouse was like a maze. They soon found themselves near a balcony overlooking the Chili Supper.

"We're cornered," said Nikki, holding up her potato masher.

Growling vegetables stalked in from all sides.

"Finally, after fattening you kids up on ice cream and pie, we can eat!" said the broccoli as it closed in on Alexander.

"No more sundaes for me!" yelled Nikki. She was about to be squished by squash.

A husk of corn pressed against Alexander, ear to ear.

"Back off, weenies!" Rip jumped between Alexander and the corn. He held up something small and red.

"A *regular* radish?" growled the corn. "Is that supposed to scare us?"

"Nope," said Rip. "But I'm guessing *she* will."

Rip dropped his radish to the floor. The veggie monsters looked down to see a long trail of radishes.

A moment later, Stermont Stella hopped into view. She picked up a radish and started nibbling.

The vegetable monsters all ran screaming from Stella.

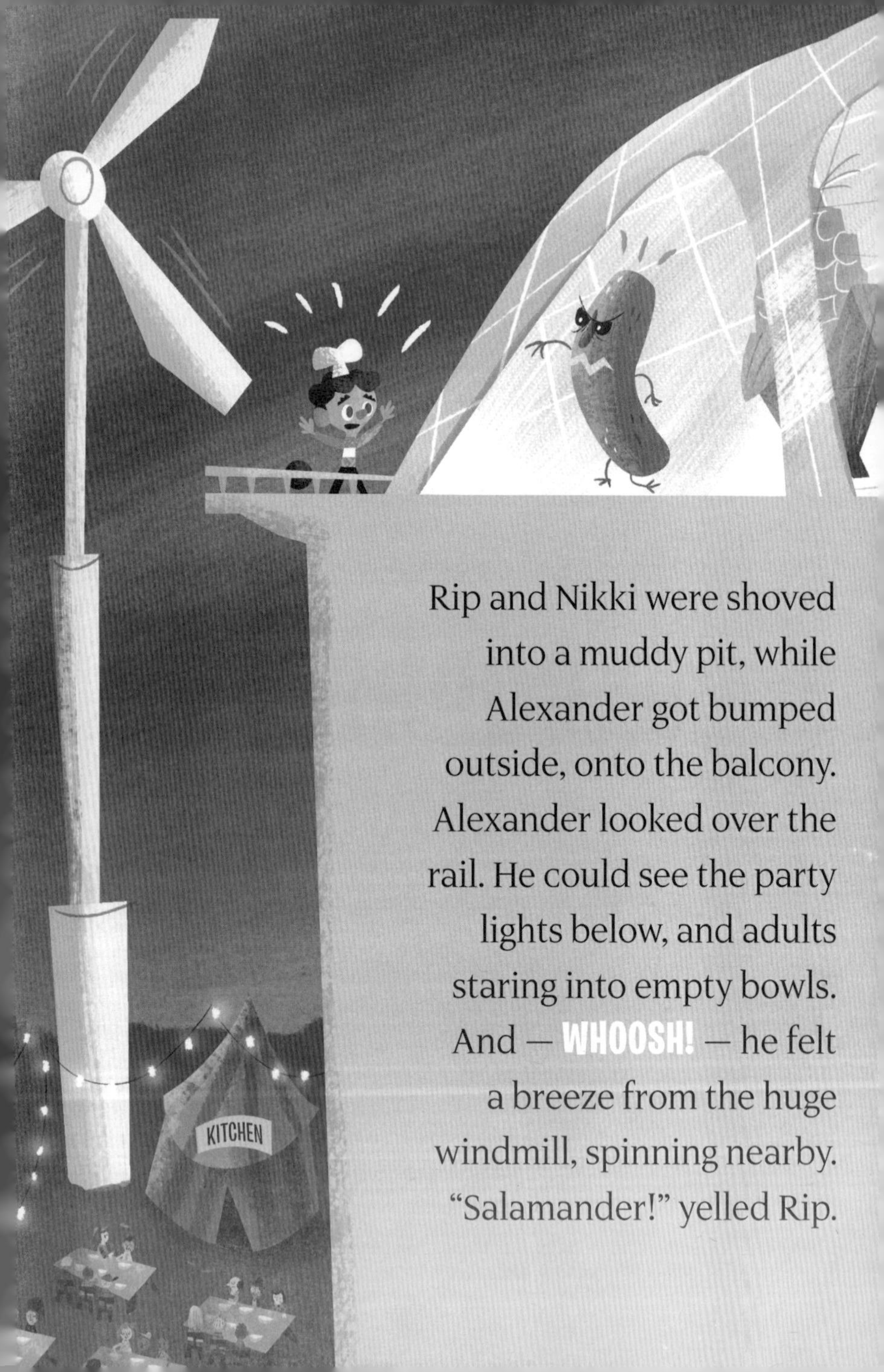

Rip and Nikki were shoved into a muddy pit, while Alexander got bumped outside, onto the balcony. Alexander looked over the rail. He could see the party lights below, and adults staring into empty bowls. And — **WHOOSH!** — he felt a breeze from the huge windmill, spinning nearby. "Salamander!" yelled Rip.

Alexander looked into the greenhouse. Stella was taking a nap! The veggies were closing in on Rip and Nikki, who were hip-deep in mud.

"Hey, veggies!" Alexander shouted from the balcony. "You've already trapped those two! Bet you can't catch me!"

A cucumber turned toward Alexander. "He's right, guys. LET'S GET HIM!"

The vegetables rushed the balcony, and, as one bunch, took a flying leap at Alexander. He took a step back, and — **WHOOP!** — slipped on a giant pea.

OOMPH! Alexander fell onto the balcony floor. Then he watched as the vegetables sailed over him. Off the balcony. Into the blades of the giant windmill.

CHAPTER 16

CHOP CHOP!

There you are, Al!" said Alexander's dad. "I've been looking for you all night."

Alexander watched his dad swallow a spoonful of chili. "*Mmmm*. Best. Veggie. Chili. EVER! What's in here, anyway?"

Alexander smiled. "A chef never shares his secrets!"

He walked to the kitchen tent.

"Mr. Hoarsely!" Alexander said. "The veggie monsters —"

"Tut-tut!" said Mr. Hoarsely. "I don't want to hear the *M*-word." He leaned in. "I thought the supper was going to be ruined, but then diced vegetables rained from the sky. I caught enough to feed everyone."

"Those veggies —"

"Nope!" Mr. Hoarsely said. "I don't want to know."

"Okay, okay," Alexander said. "Have you seen Rip and Nikki?"

"Oh, sure," said Mr. Hoarsely, "I made them wash up — they were *so* muddy!"

Alexander found his friends at the sink.

"The S.S.M.P. weeded out another monstrous plot!" said Nikki.

"Yeah," said Rip. "The best part was watching you stand up to that corn."

"Aw, shucks," said Alexander as he pulled out the notebook to make a new entry. "I couldn't have done it without you guys."

MEAT-EATING VEGETABLES

A crispy, leafy, crunchy bunch of monsters.

HABITAT Weird new greenhouse.

DIET Tender, juicy grade-schoolers.

TROY CUMMINGS

has no tail, no wings, no fangs, no claws, and only one head. As a kid, he believed that monsters might really exist. Today, he's sure of it.

BEHAVIOR This creature likes video games, but can never make it past the fire cave. (World 3, Level 2.)

HABITAT Troy Cummings lives on a hill near a neat old observatory.

DIET Blueberry pancakes with REAL maple syrup. None of that fake stuff!

EVIDENCE Few people believe that Troy Cummings is real. The only proof we have is that he supposedly wrote and illustrated *The Eensy-Weensy Spider Freaks Out!*, and *Giddy-up, Daddy!*

WARNING Keep your eyes peeled for more monsters to come!

YEAH, YEAH.

Corn and tomatoes aren't technically vegetables, but we lumped them in here anyway.

BEHAVIOR Veggie monsters pretend to be school workers so they can chill, tenderize (mash you into shape!), and fatten you up before... **CHOMP!**

WARNING!

Got a beef with the veggie monsters? Cook your way out!

* Take a dozen mixed veggie monsters
* Chop into small bits
* Heat in a pot for 20 minutes
* YUM!